RELAXING COLORING BOOK FOR ADULTS STRESS RELIEVING DESIGNS

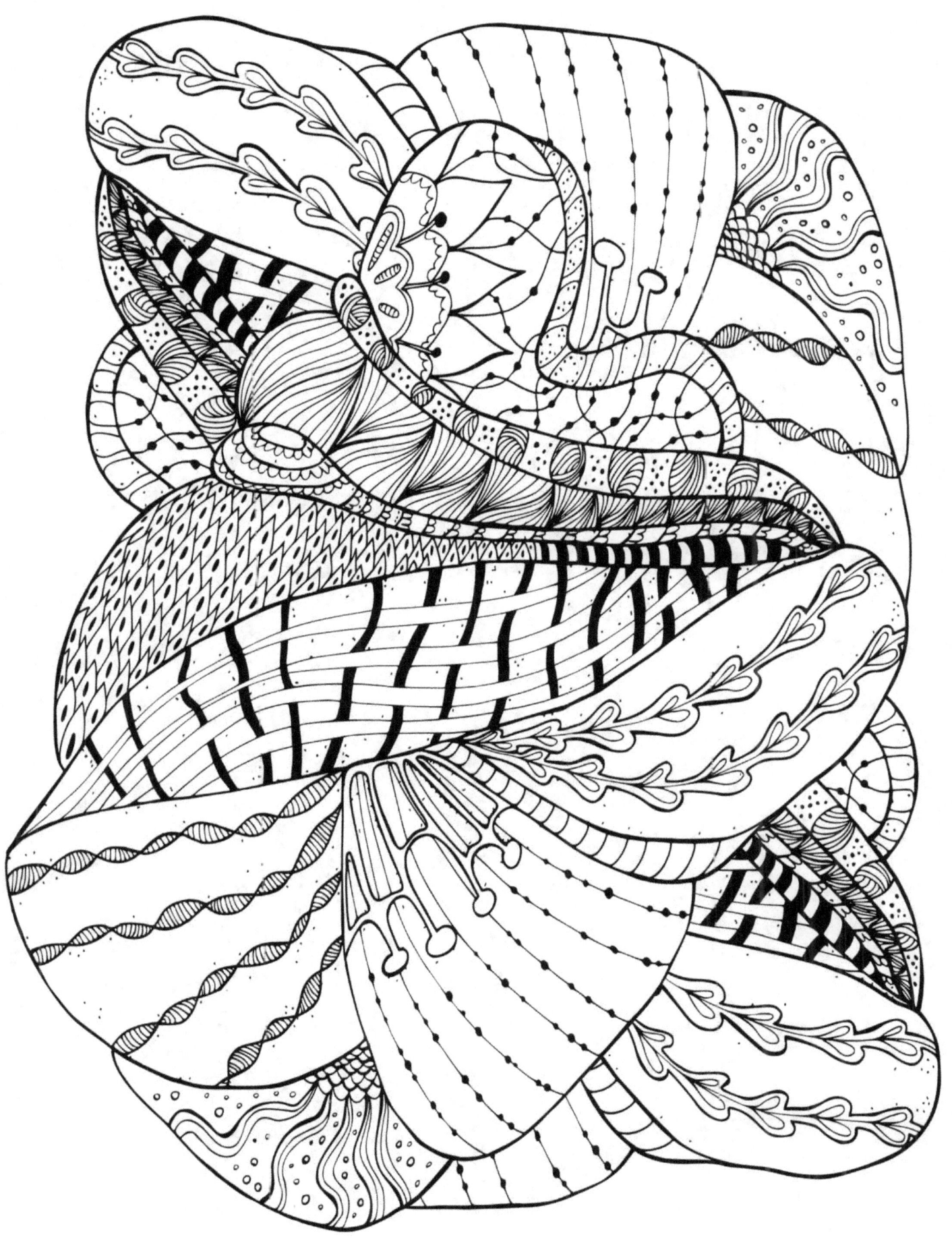

THANK YOU FOR USING THIS COLORING BOOK, WE REALLY
HOPE YOU LIKED IT. PLEASE LET US KNOW IF YOU LIKED IT
BY WRITING A REVIEW. IT MEANS A LOT TO US.

THANK YOU!

www.ingramcontent.com/pod-product-compliance
Lightning Source LLC
Chambersburg PA
CBHW080833310526

45788CB00020B/3456